Bukowski
And The Beats

M. J. Poynter

Bukowski and the Beats

A Proletarian Writer's Portrayal of the
Degradation and Exploitation of America's Working-Class

An Extended Essay on the Life and Work
of Charles Bukowski

By

M. J. Poynter

M. J. Poynter

All rights reserved.
No part of this publication may be reproduced,
distributed, or transmitted in any form or by any means
without prior permission of the author

M. J. Poynter asserts the right to be identified as the author of this work.

Copyright © M. J. Poynter, 2015

This essay is intended to be read as an academic work,
except for the use of quotations and short passages these are
the author's original ideas and all other sources
have been clearly cited and referenced.

ISBN–13: 978-1511654302
ISBN–10: 1511654309

Cover image by Writers and their Typewriters
www.xavier.edu

Produced by CreateSpace
www.CreateSpace.com

Foreword

The prosperity of Post-War America is regarded as a new age of conformity, whereby stability could be maintained with the affluence of an expanding economy. But in fact it marked the beginning of a world of stress and disorder, in which America struggled against the new global balance of power to maintain an individualist democracy against the background of the Cold War. This era seems to represent a culmination of negative forces threatening Western civilization with a sense of ultimate terror and destruction which has consequently shaped the physical, psychological and spiritual attitudes of America.

The prosperity of the Post-War years permitted commercialism to flourish on an unprecedented scale, rein-forcing a climate of consensus, conformity and complacency. The Beats were the first to express their disapproval at what they saw as the creation of a soulless America, whose lack of spiritual values and erosion of human ideals, marked a decline in freedom and individualism. As America began to experience new phenomena such as urbanization, mass communication, technological advancement and increased industrialization a psychological crisis began to emerge in the form of a dehumanized and depersonalized way of life.

While Allen Ginsberg neurotically denounced materialism and Jack Kerouac expressed his dismay at the suppression of suburbia,

M. J. Poynter

Charles Bukowski's main concerns are with the degradation and exploitation of America's workforce. The continued use of Taylor and Fordist production techniques have reduced labour to a mindless repetition, divorcing its value from the creation of wealth, while the growth of bureaucracy, increased corporate power and the decline of union influence has caused America to increasingly become a society of inequality and exclusion.

Contents

Foreword 5

Introduction 9

1. The Life and Work of Charles Bukowski 13
2. Criticisms on Charles Bukowski 16
3. The Beat Generation 24
4. The Mode of Production 32
5. The American Class Divide 41
6. The Proletarianization of Post-War America 49

Conclusion 64

Bibliography 68

About the Author 73

M. J. Poynter

Introduction

Just as the writers of the Lost Generation felt disillusioned, culturally orphaned and divested of their ideals and beliefs as a consequence of their participation in World War One, Charles Bukowski, like many other Beat writers, can be seen as a product of the Second World War.[1] Rebelling against the values of their age, these writers sought to explore new modes of expression and approach, and regarded society as suffering from a collective psychosis whose symptoms were later to manifest themselves in the form of the Cold War.[2]

As most of Bukowski's work has been written from personal experience, he becomes what Cherkovski describes as a "wise old dog," who "saw the disintegration of post-World War II American life before it began."[3] Brewer similarly argues, that Bukowski's work, "earns its understanding's, its truths, and its discoveries through a direct and honest apprehension of experience, without outside ideas imposed.[4] By persistently focussing upon America's working-class, Bukowski has anticipated and influenced much of the "dirty realism"

---

[1] Stephenson, G. *The Daybreak Boys, Essays on the Literature of the Beat Generation*. (Souther Illinois University: Carbondale and Edwardsville, 1990), p. 4.
[2] *Ibid*, p. 6.
[3] Cherkovski, N. *Bukowski, A Life*. (South Royalton: Steerforth Press, 1997), p. viii.
[4] Brewer, G. *Charles Bukowski*. (London: Twayne Publishers, 1997), p. x.

that became predominant in the 1970's and 80's, as characterised in the writings of Raymond Carver.[5]

While Jack Kerouac's *The Town and the City* (1950) and William Burroughs's *Junky* (1953) recorded horrific visions of the atomic age with their portrayal of Post-apocalyptic America, much of Bukowski's work shares the same death wish through a self-destruction of alcohol, suicide and despair.[6] In contrast to the paranoia of Soviet expansion and the threat of atomic annihilation, Bukowski depicts how valueless life has become in a society whose sense of morality has been replaced with a desire for increased industrialization, characterized by mass production, low wages and excessive bureaucracy.

Bukowski's first novel *Post Office* (1971) provides a jarring criticism of bureaucratized labour during the 1950's and 60's and portrays an America where class is unmistakably measured by money. This enables Bukowski to distinguish the working-class, as those who are damned to a life of labour, from the upper-classes enjoying an existence of leisure.[7] In writing *Factotum* (1975), Bukowski portrays working-class America during World War Two and the supposed subsequent boom years, illustrating the deadening effect of repetitive, unskilled labour.[8] While the novel *Ham on Rye* (1982) is a recollection of Bukowski's youth and upbringing, in which he rejects the family structure, and its intended labour values, and exposes the myth of social advancement through the merits of hard work.[9]

By the end of the 1950's a new generation was beginning to emerge a "mass culture" of consumption and conformity, characterized

---

[5] Brewer, G. *Charles Bukowski*. (London: Twayne Publishers, 1997), p. 6.
[6] *Ibid*, p. 174.
[7] *Ibid*, pp. 10-17.
[8] *Ibid*, pp. 17-26.
[9] *Ibid*, pp. 34-44.

by blandness and predictability.[10] The Beats rebelled against this indifferent, complacent society, believing that its lack of spiritual values and erosion of human ideals would be to the detriment of individualism.[11] By rejecting mainstream values Bukowski's writing represents a critique on urban civilization and implies a search to recover an authentic human identity. He upholds the spirit of individualism with his deadening assault on the world of work and his blatant refusal to except or comply with its principles.

The use of Scientific Management techniques and increased levels of automation has ensured America's industrial success. But despite the higher levels of education and training that are required for modern industry, Braverman deduces how the workforce has increasingly become stratified into forms of debilitating semi-skilled labour, whose petty repetitive operations have failed to sustain workers interests.[12] With personnel departments assisting in the manipulation and pacification of manpower, and consultation firms seeking to cut costs, improve efficiency and raise production levels, the workforce has consequently become alienated and de-gradated from the production process and the creation of wealth.[13]

Sharing many of the values of counter-culture idealism, Bukowski's tales of ordinary madness seem to have inspired many readers to recognise a sense of heroism within their ordinary lives.[14]

---

[10] Bradbury, M. *The Modern American Novel*. (Oxford: Oxford University Press, 1983). p. 128.

[11] Stephenson, G. *The Daybreak Boys, Essays on the Literature of the Beat Generation*. (Souther Illinois University: Carbondale and Edwardsville, 1990), pp. 6-7.

[12] Braverman, H. *Labour and Monopoly Capital, The Degradation of Work in the Twentieth Century*. (New York: Monthly Review Press, 1975), p. 305.

[13] *Ibid*, pp. 38, 87.

[14] Cherkovski, N. *Bukowski, A Life*. (South Royalton: Steerforth Press, 1997), p. viii.

By depicting the routine mundane existence of the blue-collar worker, Bukowski is able to offer an insight into American life at the lower end of the socio-economic spectrum.[15] His work serves as a critique on the social effects of Post-War industrialization with its ever increasing class divide and uneven redistribution of wealth, recognizing the Proletarianization of America's workforce before it became a recognised phenome-non.[16]

---

[15] Locklin, G. *Charles Bukowski: A Sure Bet*. (Sudbury: Water Row Press, 1996), p. 30.
[16] Cherkovski, N. *Bukowski, A Life*. (South Royalton: Steerforth Press, 1997), p. viii.

Chapter One
The Life and Work of Charles Bukowski

Charles Bukowski was born in the town of Andernach in Germany on 16 August, 1920. An only child of poor German parents, he was brought to the United States of America at the age of three where he grew up in the city of Los Angeles.[17] As a young man Bukowski held a succession of unskilled lowly paid jobs, most of which were in the service industry. These numerous forms of menial employment, offering little opportunity of stability or prosperity, would later prove invaluable in forming the basis of his poetry and in particular the contents of the novels *Factotum* (1975) and *Post Office* (1971).

As a youth Bukowski was heavily influenced by the works of Sinclair Lewis, Earnest Hemingway, D. H. Lawrence and in particular John Fante.[18] His writing exhibits a strong sense of immediacy and a refusal to embrace formal structure, earning him a place in the hearts of Beat generation readers and contributors to Underground publications. Although Bukowski has never been formally associated with bona fide Beat writers, such as, Jack Kerouac or Allen Ginsberg he is generally accepted as an "honorary" Beat.[19] Bukowski's work is

---

[17] Brewer, G. *Charles Bukowski*. (London: Twayne Publishers, 1997), p. 1.
[18] Christy, J. *The Buk Book, Musings on Charles Bukowski*. Toronto: ECW Press, 1997), pp. 16-18.
[19] Smith, G. (ed). "To Charles Bukowski – In Appreciation." *ATOM MIND*, Albuquerque: Mother Road Publications, (Summer, 1994), vol 4, no' 14, pp. 22-32.

free-formed, humorous and painfully honest, often depicting the people of the streets, such as: skid row bums, hustlers and prostitutes. By exploring elements of their transient lifestyle his work serves as a valuable critique on the American working-class experience, illustrating the problems caused by Post-War industrialization.

Charles Bukowski had a prolific writing career spanning well over thirty years. His first short story, *"Aftermath of a Lengthily Rejection Slip"* appeared in Story magazine in 1944.[20] Bukowski began writing poetry at the age of thirty-five publishing his work in small underground magazines from 1955 throughout the 1960's. By 1967 he began writing a column *Notes of a Dirty Old Man*, for the Los Angeles Alternative newspaper Open City. In 1970 he resigned from the U.S. Post Office to pursue a full-time career as a professional writer.[21] Bukowski has published over thirty-two books of poetry, five books of short stories, the screenplay to the movie *Barfly* (1987) and six novels. Some of his best known works, depicting his autobiographical character Henry Chinaski, include the critique *Post Office* (1971), examining the debilitating working conditions that exist within the bureaucracy of the United States postal service. *Factotum* (1975), which portrays Chinaski's hand-to-mouth existence as he drifts from one dead-end job to another and *Ham on Rye* (1982), a portrayal of Henry Chinaski's slum childhood of hardship and alienation, during the years of the Great Depression.

Charles Bukowski died in San Pedro, California 9 March, 1994 at the age of seventy-three, shortly after completing his last novel *Pulp* (1994). As Charles Bukowski has become one of the most influential and imitated poets of today many would consider him to be one of the America's best-known contemporary writers of poetry and

---

[20] Brewer, G. *Charles Bukowski*. (London: Twayne Publishers, 1997), p. 2.
[21] *Ibid*, p. xiv.

prose. Today his popularity appears to remain undiminished with many of his books being translated into over a dozen languages and continuing to sell worldwide. The next chapter will provide a critical analysis of Bukowski's work and consider how he rose from obscurity to become a cult figure and laureate of American low life.

M. J. Poynter

Chapter Two
Criticisms on Charles Bukowski

This chapter will provide a critical analysis of Bukowski's work as it pertains to proletarian themes of degradation and exploitation. Bukowski's portrayal of working-class experience is far removed from the intelligentsia's perceptions of American society, so despite achieving international success, Bukowski's still remains an outsider to the literary establishment. Therefore, as not many critics have taken him seriously, he has consequently become more of a cult figure as opposed to an accepted mainstream writer.

Bukowski has successfully based his writing on a combination of reworked personal experiences and myth, creating a carefree and self-destructive attitude towards life. As a solitary writer of drunkenness, vomiting and despair, Bukowski's tales of ordinary madness have inspired many readers to recognise a sense of heroism within their everyday lives. Bukowski's success can be attributed to his originality and what Jim Christy describes as "the literary trick in being himself," explaining:

> "He had been a bum, a lumpen proletarian, a drunk…but what would eventually set Bukowski apart from the rest of them – the Knut Hamsums, Jack Londons, Maxim Gorkys, and Jim Tullys – was that Bukowski was funny. Sometimes

the humour was black, sometimes it was near slapstick, but he was nearly always funny."[22]

Bukowski's use of dead pan humour certainly reflects a cynic who never fails to amuse, but his painfully honest observations of poverty, drunkenness and despair also reflect a compassionate individual who is genuinely concerned with the problems of society. The use of humour in situations that would ordinarily be very serious and distressing has enabled Bukowski's work to deal with life's adversities in a dignified manner exhibiting a sense of courage and resolve.

Gerald Locklin has described Bukowski as being at his best when "conveying life at the infrared base of the socioeconomic spectrum," and at his worst when being, "waxing pseudopoetic or pseudophilosophical."[23] Bukowski's masterful depictions of skid row with its hustlers, prostitutes and cheap rooming houses certainly does portray the underclass of America in graphic detail. But when attempting to comment upon current affairs or resorting to gratuitous sensationalism, his work often loses its integrity and becomes a cheap imitation of itself. Thus Bukowski produces his best when writing from the stability of experience. His depiction of bureaucracy and the mechanised working conditions of Post-War America offers a first-hand critique into the life of the blue collar worker.

While Locklin criticises Bukowski's earlier work for being either, "too romantic and surrealistic on the one hand" and "too uneventful on the other," Brewer argues that the surrealism of Bukowski's earlier work depicts an artist struggling for an anti-rational

---

[22] Christy, J. *The Buk Book, Musings on Charles Bukowski*. Toronto: ECW Press, 1997), pp. 24-26.
[23] Locklin, G. *Charles Bukowski: A Sure Bet*. (Sudbury: Water Row Press, 1996), p. 30.

language in order to truthfully represent his existence.[24] Brewer observes how Bukowski's later work begins to change direction moving away from surrealism and metaphor towards a concentration on narrative, dialogue and intentional mundanity, resulting in a more confessional style of writing.[25] Here Locklin supports this view explaining:

> "What should probably most be noted in the early poems is a flatness which at this stage constitutes an interesting but unutilized defect. And yet it was from this fatness, this plainness, this literal and selective exactitude that the unique and powerful directness of his major work was to emerge."[26]

Locklin admires Bukowski for developing a conversational narrative and taking poetry in a new direction.[27] Bukowski's earlier poems certainly possess a spontaneous free-form lyricism that reflects an attitude of defiance. An example of this can be seen in "poverty" taken from *Burning in Water, Drowning in Flame* (1955-73), in which Bukowski describes a "truly living man", recognised by qualities of primitive wildness.

> "I have looked almost half a century
> and he has not been seen
>
> a living man, truly alive,
> say when he brings his hands down

---

[24] Locklin, G. *Charles Bukowski: A Sure Bet*. (Sudbury: Water Row Press, 1996), p. 1.
[25] *Ibid*, pp. 90-92.
[26] *Ibid*, p. 39.
[27] Esterly, G. " Buk: The Pock-Marked Poetry of Charles Bukowski." *Rolling Stone*, (16 June, 1976), pp. 28-34.

Bukowski and the Beats

> from lighting a cigarette
> you see his eyes
> like the eyes of a tiger staring past
> into the wind."[28]

While still moving towards a conversational narrative, many of Bukowski's later works begin to show a greater sense of balance and timing. For example: in the poem "the man at the piano" taken from *Dangling in the Tournefortia* (1981), Bukowski illustrates the futile soul destroying existence of a lounge singer.

> "the man at the piano
> plays a song
> he didn't write
> sings words
> that aren't his
> upon a piano
> he doesn't own
>
> while
> people at tables
> eat, drink and talk
>
> the man at the piano
> finishes
> to no applause"[29]

---

[28] Bukowski, C. *Burning in Water Drowning in Flame: Selected Poems 1955-1973*. (Santa Rosa: Black Sparrow Press, 1974). p. 128.

[29] Bukowski, C. *Dangling in the Tournefortia*. (Santa Rosa: Black Sparrow Press, 1981). p. 278.

As a writer Bukowski remained a loner, an outsider who never wished to associate himself with any literary movement. He did not concern himself with current affairs and did not write to achieve some political end. While Henry Miller's *Tropic of Cancer* (1934) and Anaïs Nin's *Delta of Venus* (1977) set out to liberate literature often being sexually explicit and using profanity to demonstrate their cause, Bukowski was never interested in instructing the reader, instead he saw the process of writing as an act of self-discovery, a means from which to teach himself.[30] Therefore, Bukowski's emphasis on drunkenness, poverty and despair does not so much attempt to make a protest but reflect social conditions as they really are.

Bukowski's use of first person prose narrative gives his writing an effortless quality which Neeli Cherkovki likens to the leanness of Earnest Hemingway's *The Sun Also Rises* (1926), and the "gutsiness and instinctual sense of unadorned human speech" in some of Nelson Algren's writing.[31] Locklin applauds Bukowski for "leading a new direction in American poetry with his direct, spontaneous, conversational free-form style," concluding that, "many poets have been talking for a long time about getting more of a narrative quality into their work, but it was Bukowski, with seeming ease, who really succeeded."[32] By avoiding elaborate metaphors and excessive use of adjectives, Bukowski allows the intent of his writing to be relayed clearly and directly to the reader. This to many causes the writing to become dull and lifeless but it does create a simplicity which replaces misinterpretation with raw eloquence.

---

[30] Cherkovski, N. *Bukowski, A Life*. (South Royalton: Steerforth Press, 1997), p. 116.
[31] *Ibid*, p. 213.
[32] Brewer, G. *Charles Bukowski*. (London: Twayne Publishers, 1997), pp. 130-31.

Bukowski uses his autobiographical character Henry Chinaski as a social protagonist, who constantly evaluates the world in which he lives. Harrison illustrates this point describing how Bukowski creates "an increasing awareness of the dialectical nature of the relationship between the self and the other."[33] What Harrison is essentially referring to here, is that Bukowski (subject) and the world in which he lives (object), are mutually defined as a result of their interaction with one another, resulting in a (subject) that both creates and refuses the social world in which he lives. In this case Bukowski creates a morbid impression of the world of work in which Henry Chinaski is exposed to the exploitation of ruthless employers, bad working conditions and low wages, and refuses to accept this world of hierarchy, authority and domination as normal.

Bukowski's work has often been criticised for being uneven in content and style, this is possibly due to the large number of poems he wrote while being under the influence of alcohol. As he mostly wrote about his personal experiences he often repeated himself allowing much of his work to become bad imitation. In this example: Bukowski recollects the soulless futility of going into Sears-Roebuck, a large department store in "out of the mainstream" taken from *Dangling in the Tournefortia* (1981).

> "there's a blue jean sale on.
> I purchase a pair for under $10.
> I take the escalator down
> and in the candy section
> I buy a large bag of popcorn."[34]

---

[33] Harrison, R. *Against the American Dream, Essays on Charles Bukowski*. (Santa Rosa: Black Sparrow Press, 1995), pp. 47-8.
[34] Bukowski, C. *Dangling in the Tournefortia*. (Santa Rosa: Black Sparrow Press, 1981). p. 88.

Here again he creates exactly the same scenario in "time is made to be wasted":

> "I had just bought some boxer shorts
> and a pair of blue jeans
> and I had just purchased a box of popcorn
> and I was walking by the shoes dept."[35]

But in literary terms Norse explains how Bukowski "opened his veins freely and spilled blood and gore on everything," like Raymond Chandler and James M. Cain, Bukowski's hard hitting style reached those dark areas where frustration and despair were predominant.[36] His explicit world of whores, bums and drunks has gained him wide counter-culture fame, although not in the same class as William S. Burroughs or Allen Ginsberg, but nevertheless his simple honest approach has stretched across social barriers from educated professionals to the average man in the street.

The most important factor that has set Bukowski apart from other writers, with regards to style and content, has been his unwillingness to compromise himself. Bukowski has rejected form in poetry, referring to it as, "a paycheck for learning to turn the same screw that has held things together."[37] But in some ways Bukowski's unwillingness to compromise himself has worked to his advantage, prompting John Brayan, founder of the Los Angeles alternative paper Open City, to offer Bukowski a column to write virtually anything he

---

[35] Bukowski, C. *Dangling in the Tournefortia*. (Santa Rosa: Black Sparrow Press, 1981). p. 89.

[36] Norse, H. "Laughter in Hell, Charles Bukowski is Dead." *ATOM MIND*, Albuquerque: Mother Road Publications. (Summer, 1994), vol 4, no' 14, p. 65.

[37] Smith, E (ed). "Sure, the Charles Bukowski Newsletter." no' 3, 1991.

wanted.[38] Bukowski seized this opportunity and began writing short narratives, some of which were fantastic in nature, while others were fictional re-workings based upon his own personal experiences. Bukowski appears to have been successful in using this technique as a platform from which to base his entire writing career.

Despite the efforts of John Martin's Black Sparrow Press, which brought Bukowski out of obscurity and established him as a successful writer, Bukowski still remains an alienated figure in the literary world. Perhaps critics view him as a flawed writer whose portrayal of America's working-class shows little ability in establishing plot and developing character, or perhaps his emphasis on low-brow culture and his reputation as an alcoholic bum, promoting nihilist ideologies, has deterred the literary establishment from taking him too seriously. The next chapter will examine the Beat generation and consider Bukowski's relationship to beat writers and Confessional poetry.

---

[38] Harrison, R. *Against the American Dream, Essays on Charles Bukowski*. (Santa Rosa: Black Sparrow Press, 1995), p. 249.

M. J. Poynter

Chapter Three
The Beat Generation

As an outsider not wishing to be associated with any literary circle Bukowski has remained difficult to classify among his poetic contemporaries. In earlier decades Bukowski was loosely linked with the poorly defined "Meat School" poets, who according to Brewer, "wrote in tough, direct masculine manner about the concerns of the lumpenproletariat."[39] Bukowski has been described by Jack Hirschman as "the last of the alcohol poets", due to his lack of political ideology and internalized focus upon the private world of lower-class experience.[40] Marginalized as an underground poet for many years, the emergence of small-press magazines, such as, *Harlequin* and *The Outsider*, combined with the liberation of the counter-culture, helped to bring Bukowski out of obscurity and into the public domain.[41] Over time his raw simplistic and uncompromising style of writing, often using profane language and sexually explicit subject matter, would unwittingly secure his association with the Beats.

The "Beat Generation", according to Stephenson, is a term that Jack Kerouac used in a conversation with John Clellon Holmes in

---

[39] Brewer, G. *Charles Bukowski*. (London: Twayne Publishers, 1997), p. 8.
[40] Richmond, S. *Spinning off Bukowski*. (Northville: Sun Dog Press, 1996), p. 45.
[41] Brewer, G. *Charles Bukowski*. (London: Twayne Publishers, 1997), p. 3.

1948. Four year later Holmes wrote an article for The New York Times entitled "This is the Beat Generation", stating that "beat", "implies the feeling of having been used, of being raw, it involves a sort of nakedness of mind and ultimately, of souls."[42] In Kerouac's novel *On the Road* (1957) the term "beat" is used to describe the character Dean Moriarty as "he was BEAT – the root, the soul of Beatific."[43] Stephenson observes how Kerouac's novel uses the phrase Beat Generation to describe a group of disaffected young men and women with whom the author identifies.[44] Therefore, the Beats can essentially be seen as an unconventional group of writers disillusioned with the conformity and consumerism of Post-War American society. The Beats regarded society as suffering from a collective psychosis where symptoms had manifested themselves in the form of the Cold War. Feeling alienated from their own country the Beats held a romantic notion of rediscovering America in an attempt to find self-satisfaction, through writing, travelling and experimentation with drugs, alcohol, and Eastern religion, in an attempt to find spiritual fulfilment.

After Bukowski's death, "editors of major newspapers across America got the wrong idea about Bukowski," explains Richmond, "namely that he was 'King Of The Beatniks'."[45] Richmond insists that this was really a vindictive statement made by the Literary Press intended to diminish Bukowski's incomparable body of work. Christy

---

[42] Bartlett, L.(ed). *The Beats: Essays in Criticism*. (London: Mc Farland, 1981), p. 3.
[43] Kerouac, J. *On the Road*. (London: Penguin Books, 1991), p. 177.
[44] Stephenson, G. *The Daybreak Boys, Essays on the Literature of the Beat Generation*. (Souther Illinois University: Carbondale and Edwardsville, 1990), p. 2.
[45] Richmond, S. *Spinning off Bukowski*. (Northville: Sun Dog Press, 1996), p. 129.

similarly argues that, "the notion of Beatnik Buk is absurd," as in most literary circles, "Bukowski was their biggest nightmare, a horrible dream they never thought could come true," but just about anywhere else, "he was just what was wanted."[46] From these comments it becomes clear that despite Bukowski's literary success he was not accepted by the literary establishment. Russell Harrison more persuasively explains that while "superficially, Bukowski may be seen as a late-blooming confessional or a late-blooming Beat or even as a poet of the counter-culture", he is essentially a "proletarian poet, but a proletarian poet of a special sensibility, whose poetry owes something to the confessionals, the beats and the counter-culture of the 1960's."[47]

Bukowski certainly can be viewed as a proletarian poet in so far as his poetry reflects working class experiences, characterizing marginal dis-functional individuals. This effectively separates Bukowski from other Beat writers such as Jack Kerouac who constantly glorified minority figures such as the Negro. In this example taken from *On the Road* (1957), Kerouac describes an idyllic evening listening to bop musicians.

> "The third sax was an alto, eighteen-year-cool, contemplative young Charlie-Parker-type Negro from high school, with a broadgash mouth, taller than the rest, grave. He raised his horn and blew into it quietly and thoughtfully and elicited phrases and architectural Miles Davies logics. These were the children of the great bop innovators."[48]

---

[46] Christy, J. *The Buk Book, Musings on Charles Bukowski*. Toronto: ECW Press, 1997), pp. 34, 40

[47] Harrison, R. *Against the American Dream, Essays on Charles Bukowski*. (Santa Rosa: Black Sparrow Press, 1995), p. 29.

[48] Kerouac, J. *On the Road*. (London: Penguin Books, 1991), p. 217.

Bukowski and the Beats

While in comparison Bukowski does not seek to glorify minority figures, but instead depicts more realistically the relationship that exists between working-class blacks and whites, as this example from *Factotum* (1975) illustrates.

> "The rain stopped and the sun came out. I was in the black district. I walked along slowly. […] I put my suitcase down. A high yellow was sitting on the porch steps swinging her legs. She did look good.
> "Hello, poor white trash!"
> I didn't say anything. I just stood there looking at her.
> "How'd you like a piece of ass, poor white trash?"
> […] I picked up my suitcase and began to approach her up the walk. As I did I noticed a side curtain on a window to my left move just a bit. I saw a black man's face. He looked like Jersey Joe Wolcott. I backed down the pathway to the sidewalk. Her laughter followed me down the street."[49]

These insightful depictions of working-class deprivation has enabled Bukowski to become "a moral spokesman for the American lumpen-proletariat," explains Anon, "a chronicler of our urban degeneracy, whose dingy furnished rooms, drinking, and fornication's are neither bohemianism nor self-indulgence, but a way of life."[50] Bukowski's portrayal of degradation and depravity is more consistent with the pessimistic social concerns of the proletariat than the more lofty ambitions of the Beats and their romanticised view of the working man.

---

[49] Bukowski, C. *Factotum*. (London: Virgin Publishing Ltd, 1996), pp. 11-12.
[50] Harrison, R. *Against the American Dream, Essays on Charles Bukowski*. (Santa Rosa: Black Sparrow Press, 1995), p. 40.

Confessional poetry, placing a strong emphasis on personal experience, has effectively paved the way for Bukowski as it has broadened the limitations of what was considered acceptable poetic content. As Rosenthal explains, "the private life of the poet himself, especially under stress of psychological crisis," becomes a major theme.[51] Furthermore, as confessional poetry becomes a symbolic embodiment of national and cultural crisis, it can be both public and private, lyrical and rhetorical. Robert Langbaum describes confessional poetry as being "the doctrine of experience," arguing that, "the imaginative apprehension gained through immediate experience is primary and certain, whereas the analytic reflection that follows is secondary and philosophical."[52] Only part of this observation can be applied to Bukowski's work in so far as portraying personal experiences, but as most of Bukowski's work revolves around a world of isolation, whereby the poet chooses to withdrawal from the world, the philosophical element becomes limited.

There is a common resemblance between Bukowski's poetry and that of the confessionalists in that both can be described as poetry of experience. In confessional poems, such as, Robert Lowell's "Skunk Hour" there exists a symbolic embodiment of national and cultural crisis which implies a privileging of the poem's content, but Bukowski does not do this as he rejects the idea of his experience as critical or culturally symbolic. Harrison states that by not giving privilege to working-class experiences Bukowski's writing has more cultural and political significance.[53] This is somewhat debatable as Bukowski's work, although at times appearing politically antagonistic, does not

---

[51] Harrison, R. *Against the American Dream, Essays on Charles Bukowski.* (Santa Rosa: Black Sparrow Press, 1995), p. 42.
[52] *Ibid*, p. 41.
[53] *Ibid*, p. 30.

appear to make any profound political argument. Therefore, from a political perspective, Bukowski can be described as a nihilist rejecting established institutions, but not proposing any alternative solution.

Although Bukowski is indebted to the Beats and, according to Harrison, was "an admirer of Allen Ginsberg", Bukowski was nevertheless put off by the Beats as they were predominantly a middle-class, Ivy-League, bohemian elite who were detached from the labour market of the working-class.[54] In an issue of Beat Scene Bukowski stated: "The Beats…went for the media, the limelight. They slacked off on their work, their creation.[…] Fame mattered more than just doing it."[55] However, Locklin maintains, that although Bukowski does not ally himself with the Beats, he nevertheless does appear to have much in common with Jack Kerouac, in that they both opted out of World War Two, and out of the Beats, Kerouac was the one most associated with an over indulgence of alcohol. But possibly the strongest comparison that can be drawn between Bukowski and Kerouac is that they both practised spontaneous composition.[56] This example has been taken from Kerouac's novel *On the Road* (1957):

> "He invited us to his home for a bottle of beer. He lived in the tenements in back of Howard. His wife was asleep when we came in. The only light in the apartment was the bulb over her bed. We had to get up on a chair and unscrew the bulb as she lay smiling there."[57]

---

[54] Harrison, R. *Against the American Dream, Essays on Charles Bukowski.* (Santa Rosa: Black Sparrow Press, 1995), p. 41.
[55] Brewer, G. *Charles Bukowski.* (London: Twayne Publishers, 1997), p. 9.
[56] Locklin, G. *Charles Bukowski: A Sure Bet.* (Sudbury: Water Row Press, 1996), p. 5.
[57] Kerouac, J. *On the Road.* (London: Penguin Books, 1991), p. 185.

While this example has been taken from Charles Bukowski's *Ham on Rye* (1982):

> "A young girl came flouncing in, running on her high heels, long brown hair flowing behind her. She was dressed in a tight red dress. Her lips were large and expressive with excessive lipstick. She theatrically pulled her card out of the rack, punched in, and breathing with minor excitement, she put her card back in the rack."[58]

Here Kerouac's use of spontaneous composition creates a form of prose which serves both as recollection of memory and heightening casual colloquial tones in order to mimic everyday speech. While Bukowski's use of spontaneous composition has been used to return poetry to the structure of prose by rejecting traditional form which Bukowski feels constricts the writer's intentions.

While Kerouac tended to glamorize the mundane, Bukowski always retained a more gritty and cynical perspective. Christy illustrates this point explaining, that unlike Kerouac, who headed across America in search of "people who never said a commonplace thing but burned like Roman candles," Bukowski wasn't after adventure having no illusions or delusions, he "didn't care about the corn fields in Iowa, and everything anyone said was commonplace as far as he was concerned."[59] Bukowski like Kerouac and Hunter S. Thompson have become role models for people of his generation, in so far as rejecting conventional views of society, expressing an alternative opinion and attaining cult status. But as Christy explains, unlike

---

[58] Bukowski, C. *Ham on Rye*. (Santa Rosa: Black Sparrow Press, 1996), p. 204.
[59] Christy, J. *The Buk Book, Musings on Charles Bukowski*. Toronto: ECW Press, 1997), p. 19.

Bukowski and the Beats

Kerouac's image that has inspired generations of people to get on the road and experiment with composition, "the autobiographical writings of Thompson and Bukowski have got people drinking and ingesting drugs all night, and, generally acting rude."[60]

Bukowski once remarked to the editor of the Paris Metro that he felt closer to the punks than to the beatniks, proclaiming "I am not interested in this bohemian, Greenwich Village, Parisian bullshit. Algiers, Tangiers…that's all romantic claptrap."[61] But as a writer whose work reflects many values of counter-culture idealism Bukowski has come to be regarded as an "Honorary" Beat writer who found a place in the hearts of Beat generation and the contributors to small underground publications. In the next chapter Marxist theory will be examined with regards to the Mode of Production and the extent to which this determines the character of social and political life. The purpose of this analysis will be to help clarify the central arguments of Marxist ideology as it relates to this study before moving onto to examine themes of class division and the proletarianization of post-war America.

---

[60] Christy, J. *The Buk Book, Musings on Charles Bukowski*. Toronto: ECW Press, 1997), p. 56.
[61] Cherkovski, N. *Bukowski, A Life*. (South Royalton: Steerforth Press, 1997), p. 298.

M. J. Poynter

Chapter Four
The Mode of Production

In attempting to describe politics in scientific terms, Karl Marx developed a materialist conception of History, seeking to emphasise the importance of economic life and the conditions under which people produced their means of subsistence.[62] From this perspective, Marx can be seen as an economic determinist, arguing, that a society's economic structure determines the character of its social and political life.[63] Therefore, by understanding the nature of a society's economic structure one can appreciate the manner in which its ideologies are implemented, as "the history of humanity," states Marx in *German Ideology* (1846), "must always be studied and treated in relation to the history of industry and exchange."[64]

Marx argued that as a society's economic base determines its social and political life so historical developments can be explained in terms of economic class friction, in which the driving force of historical change becomes a process of interaction between forces whose internal contradictions reflect class antagonism.[65] Therefore, "the history of all hitherto existing societies," states Marx in *The*

---

[62] Heywood, A. *Politics*. (London: MacMillan Press Ltd, 1997), pp. 14, 51.
[63] McNaughton, N. *Success in Politics, A Comparative Study for Advanced Level*. (London: John Murray Publishers Ltd, 1996), p. 310.
[64] *Ibid*, p. 310.
[65] Heywood, A. *Politics*. (London: MacMillan Press Ltd, 1997), pp. 51-2.

Communist Manifesto (1848), "is the history of class struggles," suggesting that politics, together with other aspects of life, such as, law, philosophy and religion, all become part of a superstructure which is determined by an economic base.[66] As the political process seeks to work out tensions and conflict, which is rooted in the mode of production arising from the institution of private property, Marx argued, the all phenomena, such as, religious conflicts, civil wars and revolutions are merely reflections of economic and material conflict.[67] Therefore, Marx observed History from the view of the exploited classes, claiming that other historians merely observed superficial changes and often explained History in such a manner as to justify the position of the ruling class.[68]

By studying the process of historical change, Marx argued that observable events moved in discernible cycles or epochs. At the beginning of these cycles economic relationships did not contain conflict as a state of harmony existed between the organisation of production and distribution, creating a sense of social stability characteristic to that of ancient Greece.[69] However, as these societies mature they develop internal conflicts, resulting from a separation of interests, causing the emergence of class divisions. Marx recognised that there would be a small dominant ruling class which would exploit a larger producing class, at first the producing class believes itself to be benefiting from the economic system, but as exploitation increases and intensifies, the exploited class becomes aware of its true situation, resulting in growing social conflict. This creates what Marx described

---

[66] Marx, K. & Engels, F. *The Communist Manifesto.* (London: Penguin Books, 1985), p. 79.
[67] Heywood, A. *Politics.* (London: MacMillan Press Ltd, 1997), pp. 178-9
[68] McNaughton, N. *Success in Politics, A Comparative Study for Advanced Level.* (London: John Murray Publishers Ltd, 1996), p. 311.
[69] *Ibid*, p. 311.

as "dialectical materialism",[70] whereby the ruling class is confronted by the exploited class whose material interests have become dialectically opposed to that of its own, eventually conflict becomes so intense that the system collapses and has to be replaced, as in the French Revolution of 1789.

As the mode of production in material life necessitates the existence of private property social divisions will begin to emerge. From this Marx identified two opposing economic groups: the bourgeoisie (capitalist), who controls the means of production, such as factories, mines and banks; and the proletariat (working-class), who, not owning the means of production, subsist through selling their labour to the bourgeoisie in exchange for wages.[71] According to McNaughton, Marx also identified a smaller class of petit bourgeois, consisting of those who earn an independent living, such as, craftsmen, professionals, tradesmen and merchants. However, these were relatively insignificant and would be absorbed into one of the other classes, as antagonism intensified due to the capitalist system becoming more productive.[72]

While having economic power through the ownership of wealth, Marx recognised that the capitalist exercised political power through the agency of the state, arguing that the state acts as an agent of the ruling class as its main purpose is to maintain class rule.[73] Writing during a time of before universal suffrage, when voting rights were reserved for those who had wealth and property, Marx argued that democracy operated under the guise of capitalist rule, proclaiming in *German Ideology* (1846), that "the State is the form in which the

---

[70] McNaughton, N. *Success in Politics, A Comparative Study for Advanced Level*. (London: John Murray Publishers Ltd, 1996), p. 311.
[71] *Ibid*, pp. 312-13.
[72] *Ibid*, pp. 312-13.
[73] Heywood, A. *Politics*. (London: MacMillan Press Ltd, 1997), p. 52.

individuals of a ruling class assert their common interests."[74] From this perspective Marx saw democracy as a charade, as the state, with its bureaucracy, legal system, armed forces and police were truly permanent instruments of class rule, maintaining the status quo in order to ensure the continued oppression of the working-class.[75]

Due to the systematic exploitation of capitalism an irreconcilable conflict exists between the capitalist and the worker, i.e. as value is derived from the labour expended in the production of goods, the quest for profit forces capitalist enterprise to extract surplus value from their workers by paying them less than the value of their labour, this according to Heywood, causes capitalism to become "inherently unstable, because the proletariat cannot be permanently reconciled to exploitation and oppression."[76] As the capitalist system operates in such a manner, the worker is paid only a fraction of the true value of his own production, the rest becomes a surplus which is taken by the capitalist as profit. "As the productive capacity of capitalism increases," explains McNaughton, so "the value of workers' output grows," and the amount of surplus also increases, but the worker does not benefit, as wages are determined in a free market, causing workers to compete with each other for scarce jobs and so enabling employers to pay low wages.[77] Marx observe how a permanent pool of unemployed people are maintained to ensure low wage levels, so consequently, even as workers' productivity increase wages do not. This eventually results in an ever widening gap in living standards

---

[74] McNaughton, N. *Success in Politics, A Comparative Study for Advanced Level*. (London: John Murray Publishers Ltd, 1996), p. 314.
[75] *Ibid*, p. 314.
[76] Heywood, A. *Politics*. (London: MacMillan Press Ltd, 1997), p 52.
[77] McNaughton, N. *Success in Politics, A Comparative Study for Advanced Level*. (London: John Murray Publishers Ltd, 1996), p. 313.

between classes causing the proletariat to realise the nature of their exploitation and ultimately seek to overthrow the ruling class.[78]

The capitalist mode of production determines the general character of social life by reducing labour to a mere commodity, creating a depersonalised activity in which workers feel alienated from the product of their labour, their fellow workers and from themselves as creative beings.[79] As the division of labour seeks to make the production process more specialised the worker is further separated from what he is producing and consequently becomes more alienated.[80] Therefore, in *Economic and Philosophical Manuscripts* (1844), Marx states how the worker, "feels himself at home only during his leisure, whereas at work he feels homeless. His work is not voluntary but imposed, forced labour."[81] Consequently Marx saw alienation as the principal evil of capitalism, in which the worker, having no interest in the goods he is producing and no control over the production process or the financial rewards, becomes increasingly disillusioned.[82]

Marx argued that capitalism would pass through a serious crisis of overproduction creating a revolutionary class consciousness in which the workers would seize control of the means of production.[83] He was of the opinion that through a common experience of exploitation a class consciousness would develop, enabling the workers to recognise that there was more to bind them than to divide them, encouraging the formation of trade unions, frequently of strikes,

---

[78] McNaughton, N. *Success in Politics, A Comparative Study for Advanced Level*. (London: John Murray Publishers Ltd, 1996), p. 313.
[79] Heywood, A. *Politics*. (London: MacMillan Press Ltd, 1997), p. 52.
[80] McNaughton, N. *Success in Politics, A Comparative Study for Advanced Level*. (London: John Murray Publishers Ltd, 1996), p. 313.
[81] *Ibid*, p. 314.
[82] McNaughton, N. *Success in Politics, A Comparative Study for Advanced Level*. (London: John Murray Publishers Ltd, 1996), p. 313.
[83] Heywood, A. *Politics*. (London: MacMillan Press Ltd, 1997), p. 52.

demonstrations and political agitation.[84] As capitalism suffered from a tendency to over-produce, a series of booms and slumps would create periods of falling profits, unemployment and declining wages, causing the worker to become discontented. While the intense competition for scarce markets among capitalist states would lead to countries either unifying, such as, in Germany (1818-71) and Italy (1859-71), or it would lead to the creation of vast colonial empires so as to secure overseas markets.[85]

Controlling world markets would ultimately result in rivalry, conflicts and war, whereby the working classes would effectively defend a system which sought to exploit them, examples illustrating Marx's claim include the Franco-Prussian War (1870-71), and World War One (1914-18).[86] But Marx also predicted that a proletarian revolution would usher in a transitionary socialist period, during which the dispossessed capitalist would be restrained from a counter-revolution by a proletarian dictatorship. Later this dictatorship would be replaced by a communist society when class antagonisms had faded away, resulting in wealth being owned in common by all, and enabling commodity production to be replaced by production of use that would seek to satisfy genuine human needs.[87] With this, Heywood argues, the "prehistory of man would come to an end, allowing human beings for the first time to shape their own destinies and realise their full potential.[88]

When considering how applicable the mode of production in material life has been in determining the character of social and

---

[84] McNaughton, N. *Success in Politics, A Comparative Study for Advanced Level*. (London: John Murray Publishers Ltd, 1996), p. 315.
[85] *Ibid*, p. 315.
[86] *Ibid*, p. 315.
[87] *Ibid*, pp. 315-6.
[88] Heywood, A. *Politics*. (London: MacMillan Press Ltd, 1997), p. 52

political events, evidence suggests, that prior to writing *The Communist Manifesto* (1848), Marx was already an enthusiastic supporter of the Chartist struggle in England and a determined opponent of the militant traits in the German workers movement.[89] Marx called on the communists to support the Chartists in England and the agrarian reformers in America, as although none of these movements intended a revolution against capitalism, both aimed at improving working conditions through reforming the capitalist system.[90] Cohen remarks, how on a number of occasions during the 1850's, "Marx spoke in favour of the Chartist movement and a shortened working day."[91] But although he supported these campaigns and strikes to improve working conditions, he was not purely in favour of worker success in material terms but how "the association and organisation of the working-class emerging through struggle gave it the capacity to wage revolutionary battle."[92] Therefore, the real struggle was not over wages and conditions, but over power, argued Marx, believing that the real function of the Chartists would only be realised after economic crisis, in which the working-class would wake up after six years of apathy and be redirected towards the ideology of a political struggle.

Cohen argues, that due to Marx's expectation, that a "bourgeois revolution of progressive character involved the identification of capitalism with the development of industry," he had to make a distinction between productive capital and financial capital, so as to establish that economics had the power to influence the

---

[89] Cohen, A. "Divided Capitalism and Marx's Concepts of Politics." *Political Studies*, Oxford: Blackwell Publishers, (March, 1995), vol 43, no' 1, p. 94.
[90] *Ibid*, p. 94.
[91] *Ibid*, p. 97.
[92] *Ibid*, p. 97.

political.[93] In *Class Struggles in France* (1850), Marx observed how, "it was not the French bourgeoisie that ruled under Louis Phillippe, but one faction of it: bankers, stock exchange kings, railway kings...the so-called aristocracy." He argued that the industrial capitalist was excluded from political power, being represented only as a minority in the Chambers, because the enrichment of the financial aristocracy involved the impoverishment of all other classes including that of the industrial capitalist.[94] Therefore, by comparing the Silesian weavers' revolt of 1844 with French and English uprisings, Marx praised the former because "while all other movements were aimed primarily only against the owner of the industrial enterprise, the visible enemy, this movement is at the same time directed against the banker, the hidden enemy."[95]

By recognising the division between the economic and the political, Marx proposed that a centralisation of credit would place the control of finances in the hands of the state. In the tenth clause of the *Demands of the Communist Party in Germany* (1848), he called for the creation of "a State bank whose paper issues are legal tender (and which) shall replace all private banks."[96] This would effectively bring about a gradual substitution of gold and silver for paper notes, cheapening the means of exchange and bringing an end to the rule of large financial magnates in favour of all productive forces as a whole. Finally, Marx adds "this measure is necessary in order to bind the interest of the conservative bourgeoisie (the industrial capitalist) to the

---

[93] Cohen, A. "Divided Capitalism and Marx's Concepts of Politics." *Political Studies*, Oxford: Blackwell Publishers, (March, 1995), vol 43, no' 1, p. 94.
[94] *Ibid*, p. 98.
[95] *Ibid*, p. 94.
[96] *Ibid,* p. 95.

cause of the revolution."[97] But although Marx's view was to change following the revolutions of 1848, in which he refuted his earlier proposals for state intervention into the money markets, the distinction between industrial and financial capital was an essential part of his concept of politics.

On reflection it would appear that Marx's views on history and politics were constantly revised in the light of new knowledge and political events, and consequently the original vision as outlined in *The Communist Manifesto* (1848), appears to be discarded, both by the changes he made to economic theories and by the recognition of various circumstances which followed the failure of the 1848 revolutions.[98] Furthermore, the destruction of the Soviet political system, which Mikhail Gorbachev set into motion during the late 1980's, has caused communist regimes to be replaced by more liberal democratic forms of government.[99] However, the realization of a working-class consciousness, establishing the connection between the economic and the political, still remains a goal for Marxist intellectuals. Today the aspirations of communism appear to have been consigned to the history books, but whether it shall re-emerge again in the future still remains an open question?

---

[97] Cohen, A. "Divided Capitalism and Marx's Concepts of Politics." *Political Studies*, Oxford: Blackwell Publishers, (March, 1995), vol 43, no' 1, p. 95.
[98] Evans, M. (1975). *Karl Marx, Political Thinkers no' 3*. (London: George Allen & Unwin Ltd, 1975), p. 164, 168.
[99] McNaughton, N. *Success in Politics, A Comparative Study for Advanced Level*. (London: John Murray Publishers Ltd, 1996), p. 322.

Chapter Five
The American Class Divide

Most American's appear very reluctant to admit that America has a class structure. This is possibly due to the fact that America has been traditionally viewed as a rapidly expanding economy with low class barriers producing upward social mobility.[100] American idealism is also very heavily dependent upon Benjamin Franklin's description of the "American Dream" with its principle features, of Economic success, signified by a rise from rags to riches, which Franklin describes as, "the rise from impotence to importance, from dependence to independence." A "philosophy of individualism," which inferred that an individual's actions are of his own making and not determined by forces that are larger than that of himself, and finally, a "philosophy of hope" and optimism, which causes the existence of a class structure, with its social divisions of inequality, all the more difficult to accept.[101] Americans generally do not like to be reminded of a class structure as it leaves their system without the distinguishing moral character upon which its society's values appear to be based.

The first two decades after the Second World War marked a period of relative stability and vast economic growth for the U.S.

---

[100] Harrison, R. *Against the American Dream, Essays on Charles Bukowski*. (Santa Rosa: Black Sparrow Press, 1995), p. 12.
[101] *Ibid*, pp. 13-14.

economy. By the 1960's the existing class structures began breaking down as the progressive liberal attitudes of the Supreme Court and the civil rights movement, encouraged an end to racial segregation and the creation of a more equal society. But by the 1970's class barriers had risen upward and social mobility was beginning to decrease, effectively this caused the middle-class to decrease in both relative and absolute terms.[102] Over the coming decades the U.S. economy became less competitive, with a decrease in the standard of living and the redistribution of wealth primarily moving upwards, resulting in an increasing number of Americans no longer being assured of the material affluence that previous generations had once taken from granted.

Interestingly Bukowski's formal education had taken him through two years at Los Angeles City College where he majored in art and journalism, leaving without a degree in 1941, had he continued his education and completed a bachelor's degree, he would have been assured (in the 1940's) of entry into a middle-class profession.[103] However, he did not do this and instead spent fifteen years doing casual jobs, most of which were in the service sector as well as a career in the post office, leaving him with a profound understanding of the conditions of America's working-class.

Bukowski's own experiences have aided his masterful portrayal of the blue-collar worker illustrating the way in which inequalities in wealth have resulted in a world of hardship, anxiety and social exclusion. In his novel *Ham on Rye* (1982), he continually draws the reader's attention to the existence of poverty and class division. For example: Henry Chinaski recalls how, "I was not allowed to play with

---

[102] Harrison, R. *Against the American Dream, Essays on Charles Bukowski.* (Santa Rosa: Black Sparrow Press, 1995), p. 12.
[103] *Ibid*, p. 69.

Bukowski and the Beats

other children, "They are bad children," said my father, "their parents are poor." "Yes," agreed my mother. My parents wanted to be rich so they imagined themselves rich."[104] From this early childhood experience Bukowski illustrates how his character Chinaski is excluded from his peer group due to his parent's anxieties over poverty and class.

By the 1950's developments in state roadbuilding and housing policies enabled the middle-classes to acquire consumer durables such as automobiles and suburban houses, this made their relatively high positions in occupational hierarchy very visible and marked a difference in lifestyle from that of the working-class.[105] Although Bukowski's novel *Ham on Rye* (1982) is set during the Depression years of the 1930's moving up until the outbreak of the Second World War, his criticisms of affluence appear to have more in common with that of the 1950's. For example, Henry Chinaski's first impression of High School clearly reflects the class divide between himself and the other students:

> "The first day we rode our bikes to Chelsey and parked them. It was a terrible feeling. Most of those kids, at least all the older ones, had their own automobiles, many of them new convertibles, and they weren't black or dark blue like most cars, they were bright yellow, green, orange and red. [...] Everybody was nicely dressed, the guys and the girls, they had pullover sweaters, wrist watches and the latest in shoes. [...] And there was I in my home-made shirt, my one ragged pair of pants, my rundown shoes, and I was covered

---

[104] Bukowski, C. *Ham on Rye*. (Santa Rosa: Black Sparrow Press, 1996), p. 27.
[105] Woodiwiss, A. *Postmodernity USA, The Crisis of Social Modernism in Post-war America*. (London: SAGE Publications, 1993), p. 31.

> in boils. [...] Since all the guys had cars Baldy and I were ashamed of our bicycles. We left them at home and walked to school and back, two-and-one-half miles each way. We carried brown bag lunches. But most of the other students didn't even eat in the school cafeteria. They drove to malt shops with the girls, played the juke boxes and laughed. They were on their way to U.S.C."[106]

Here Bukowski's recollection of the other students with their consumer goods such as, automobiles, wrist watches and the latest shoes, combined with visions of malt shops and duke boxes, creates a stereotypical almost mocking image of American culture. While in contrast, the image of Chinaski, dressed in his home-made shirt, ragged pants and rundown shoes clearly emphasises exclusion and divisions of affluence. Due to increased middle-class affluence greater numbers of people become eligible for credit, enabling them to acquire goods of increased wealth and status, while in comparison the working-classes, not having as much disposable income or collateral, were not eligible for credit and maintained what Marx described as a "traditional standard of life," continuing to purchase goods of practical necessity.[107]

Throughout *Ham on Rye* (1982) Bukowski shows the oppressive divisions of status and hierarchy existing within education and the work place. For example: although Chinaski's father has sent his son to an affluent high school, in order to receive a better education and improve his prospects of employment, Chinaski feels despondent

---

[106] Bukowski, C. *Ham on Rye*. (Santa Rosa: Black Sparrow Press, 1996), pp. 125-6.
[107] Woodiwiss, A. *Postmodernity USA, The Crisis of Social Modernism in Post-war America.* (London: SAGE Publications, 1993), p. 31.

when discovering the relationship between hierarchy and poverty, explaining:

> "He had sent me to that rich high school hoping that the ruler's attitude would rub off on me as I watched the rich boys screech up in their cream-coloured coupes and pick up the girls in bright dresses. Instead I learned that the poor usually stay poor. That the young rich smell the stink of the poor and learn to find it a bit amusing."[108]

Bukowski also illustrates how divisions of status and hierarchy in the work place have encouraged oppressive behaviour and inequality among workers, while employed as a stockclerk at Mears-Starbuck:

> "The caste system was an accepted fact. There wasn't a single salesclerk who spoke to a stockclerk outside of a perfunctory word or two. [...] Was it possible that the salesclerks were more intelligent than the stockclerks? They certainly dressed better. It bothered me that they assumed that their station meant so much."[109]

According to Woodiwiss, by the 1960's young middle-class Americans fuelled by the protest of the civil rights movement, the Beats and the counter-culture, began to acknowledge proletarian status.[110] They criticized extended forms of family such as the work place and education for their repression of woman, sexuality and the manipulation of childhood. Education was seen as a mechanism for the

---

[108] Bukowski, C. *Ham on Rye*. (Santa Rosa: Black Sparrow Press, 1996), p. 193.
[109] *Ibid*, p. 210.
[110] Woodiwiss, A. *Postmodernity USA, The Crisis of Social Modernism in Post-war America*. (London: SAGE Publications, 1993), p. 94.

preparation of society rather than self-development, while the consumer culture began to be seen as a fetish, pacifying the human mind and being racist in intent.[111] Under these conditions the constrained life of the wage-worker began to be recognised as the cost behind the American dream.

One of the reasons why Bukowski has not been greatly received in America is that readers of serious literature have found themselves confronted with a world that conflicts with their own established ideas. In other words, a world that depicts the debilitating exploitation of the working class as portrayed through the values of lowbrow culture.[112] Readers of "serious literature" appear unable to accept that living conditions for many American people can possibly be so grim, due to the fact that America is regarded as being an economic superpower. This is possibly why Bukowski has received far greater acceptance in Europe, and in particular Germany, as his critique on American society can be more appreciated in countries where class is an acknowledged phenomenon.[113]

Russell Harrison's *Against the American Dream* (1995), explains how Bukowski has denied being a product of the American dream in two ways: "first by his unrelenting assault on deadening, routinized work as it exists for the vast majority of Americans" and secondly "by his decidedly anti-consumerist trait."[114] An example supporting Harrison's first claim has been taken from the novel *Factotum* (1975), in which Henry Chinaski is offered a job but then refuses it.

---

[111] Woodiwiss, A. *Postmodernity USA, The Crisis of Social Modernism in Post-war America.* (London: SAGE Publications, 1993), p. 94.
[112] Harrison, R. *Against the American Dream, Essays on Charles Bukowski.* (Santa Rosa: Black Sparrow Press, 1995), pp. 15-16.
[113] *Ibid*, p. 16.
[114] *Ibid*, p. 13.

"Hey, BUDDY!"
I stopped and turned.
"You want a job?"
I walked back to where he stood. Over his shoulder I could see a large dark room. There was a long table with men and women standing on both sides of it. They had hammers with which they pounded objects in front of them. In the gloom the objects appeared to be clams. They smelled like clams. I turned and continued walking down the street."[115]

While this example, "out of the mainstream", taken from *Dangling in the Tournefortia* (1995), supports Harrison's second claim, in which Bukowski recollects going into a large department store.

"I buy a large bag of popcorn
then I stroll through the hardware section
looking at tools that I have no interest in,
then to the electrical section
where I stand looking at a series of
sunlamps,
jamming the popcorn into my mouth
and feeling like a total
asshole."[116]

There exists within Bukowski's work an ethos to reject consumerism by refusing to buy clothes, gadgets, new cars and to live on credit. By effectively rejecting this social trend of increased consumption for the sake of increased consumption Bukowski's work directly clashes with the ethos on which America and other capitalist societies are based.

---

[115] Bukowski, C. *Factotum*. (London: Virgin Publishing Ltd, 1996), p. 13.
[116] Bukowski, C. *Dangling in the Tournefortia*. (Santa Rosa: Black Sparrow Press, 1981). p. 88.

M. J. Poynter

Bukowski's work has essentially exposed the price of the American Dream illustrating how individual accumulation of wealth is not possible in a system with inbuilt exclusion and inequality. His portrayal of America's underbelly depicts a stressful world of poverty and desperation in which individuals have become oppressed under a system which seeks to liberate. By pulling back the layers of hypocrisy he reveals the true cost of encouraging high profits and increased consumption at the expense of maintaining low wages, resulting in an ever more widening gap between rich and poor with the inevitable creation of a class divide. In the final chapter the proletarianization of Post-War America will be examined in relation to themes of degradation and the exploitation of America's working-class.

Bukowski and the Beats

Chapter Six
The Proletarianization of Post-War America

By the turn of the century early forms of social literature such as, Upton Sinclair's *The Jungle* (1970), Jack London's *The Iron Heel* (1908) and Theodore Dreiser's *An American Tragedy* (1925), provided vivid images of work, but the treatment of work did not focus upon the exploitation of the American working-class. It was only until the 1930's, with the publication of Jack Conroy's *The Disinherited* (1933) and John Steinbeck's *The Grapes of Wrath* (1939), with its moving depictions of exploited workers and the unemployment caused by the Great Depression, that the treatment of the working-class experience really began to receive some expression.[117] But what makes Bukowski's novels *Post Office* (1971) and *Factotum* (1975) so distinctive in contrast, is that they reflect the changes that have taken place in America since the Second World War, providing a depiction of American working-class life from 1940 to 1970.

Due to vast amounts of military spending, American industries were revived during the Second World War and this enabled Post-War America to become a land of unprecedented affluence. Bradbury describes, how "in a short time real incomes doubled and the United States became the exemplary consumer economy," this to many

---

[117] Harrison, R. *Against the American Dream, Essays on Charles Bukowski.* (Santa Rosa: Black Sparrow Press, 1995), pp. 123-4.

49

intellectuals caused the 1950's and 60's to appear as a new age of conformity, in which stability could be maintained by the affluence of an expanding economy.[118] But in fact it was marked with the disorders of the modern world, in which America struggled against the new global balance of power to maintain an individualistic capitalist democracy against a background of the Cold War. This period of affluence and individualism also saw the emergence of a better educated worker, who having a greater sense of expectation than that of his predecessor, was not afraid to speak out and act independently.

The previously mentioned writers did not glorify work and illustrate how the worker was being exploited, either by having to work too hard or simply by not being paid enough, yet they never questioned the very act of working, appearing to regard it as a necessary effort in order to attain wealth. One reviewer for the Communist paper the New Masses, complained: "it is a pity that so many writers from the proletariat can make no better use of their working-class experience than as material for introspective and febrile novels."[119] But in comparison, Bukowski's novels, like Harvey Swados' *On the Line* (1957), not only bare a negative depiction of all aspects of work, they also question whether or not work has any real usefulness at all.[120] Bukowski nearly always depicts work as being senseless and degrading, in addition to the worker being unfairly exploited. In the novel *Factotum* (1975) Bukowski repeatedly creates the image of the assembly line worker or the modest shipping clerk, trapped in his station never aspiring to any real level of prosperity. It is from this outlook of despondency and futility that Bukowski's work displays radical intentions conflicting with the very essence of American principles. As Harrison notes Bukowski's "...refusal of work...is an

---

[118] Bradbury, M. *The Modern American Novel*. (Oxford: Oxford University Press, 1983). pp. 102-3.
[119] *Ibid*, pp. 102-3.
[120] Harrison, R. *Against the American Dream, Essays on Charles Bukowski*. (Santa Rosa: Black Sparrow Press, 1995), p. 125.

implicit call for its abolition."[121] This effectively goes against the traditional values upholding American society and the notion that prosperity can be achieved through the efforts of one's own labour.

In the middle of the 19th century there had been some movement in the United States to reduce the working day in response to the increased intensity of work. As America became more Capital and technology-intensive individuals such as Benjamin Hunnicutt foresaw the potential to reduce man-hours and create higher wages. To some extent this was achieved if one considers the comments of the historian Gabriel Kolko who explains: "until 1919 capital investment was geared, unprecedentedly, to utilizing technological innovations to replace labour, and the man-hours worked as ratio of manufacturing output fell by almost one-half between 1900 and 1929." Kolko goes on to explain, that "American industry created a rhythm of life and an extraordinarily discipline and numbing division of labour which made possible a higher standard of living even as it demanded more exhausting and alienating labour."[122] This trend continued to make progress into the 1930's and the early days of Roosevelt's New Deal. The crisis of the 1930's Depression and the increases in technological efficiency promoted the idea of shorter hours as a means of providing work for a greater number of people. But Roosevelt wanted to encourage full employment and increased productivity to ensure America's economic recovery from the Depression and this consequently defeated the idea of reducing levels of work. Eventually the Second World War enabled the American economy to be pulled out of the depression and was to be followed by a period of continued economic prosperity during the 1950's.[123] Therefore, it was not until

---

[121] Harrison, R. *Against the American Dream, Essays on Charles Bukowski*. (Santa Rosa: Black Sparrow Press, 1995), p. 127.

[122] *Ibid*, p. 126.

[123] Bradbury, M. *The Modern American Novel*. (Oxford: Oxford University Press, 1983). p. 126.

the 1960's that the issue of work and alienated labour began to be widely discussed again.

In reacting against the mass society of post-war America, novels such as, Henry Miller's *The Air Conditioned Nightmare* (1945) and Ken Kesey's *One Flew Over the Cuckoo's Nest* (1962), examined various forms of bureaucracy and extended government power, questioning the individual's ability to resist these external forms of government control. Ralph Ellison's *Invisible Man* (1952) and James Purdy's *Colour of Darkness* (1957), created frightening images of alienation and lost identity, in which characters either became a formless mass or were simply impossible to recollect.[124] The theme of lost identity and drug addiction is explored in William S. Burroughs' *Junky* (1953) and *The Naked Lunch* (1959). These novels are not merely about drug addiction, but "the different ways human identity is devoured in the modern world," observes Tanner, and serves to illustrate how the individual has become "dissolved or pre-empted by nameless forces radically antipathetic to the human image."[125] Here Burroughs appears to recognise the effects of containment culture, in which people have become trapped in a large social experiment from which there is no escape. In recognising the symptoms of society's illness, Burroughs' novels effectively illustrate how society has succumb to the external forces of corporatism, bureaucracy and extended forms of government control.

Charles Bukowski's *Post Office* (1971) not only reflects the institution of work within the U.S. Post Office but also the institutions of bureaucracy within the United States itself. Therefore, *Post Office* is essentially a critique on the persistence of Taylor and Fordist management techniques that have survived into the 1950's and 60's.[126]

---

[124] Tanner, T. *City of Words, A Study of American Fiction in the Mid-Twentieth Century.* (London: Jonathan Cape, 1976), p. 18, 85.
[125] *Ibid*, p. 113.
[126] Harrison, R. *Against the American Dream, Essays on Charles Bukowski.* (Santa Rosa: Black Sparrow Press, 1995), p. 131.

Frederic Winslow Taylor's publication on *The principles of Scientific Management* (1911), sets out a vision of how management could increase levels of output by dividing labour into specific areas of production. This has resulted in the de-skilling and transforming of mental activities into purely physical labour, having the effect of reducing work into a mindless form of repetition.[127] Evidence supporting this was produced by a Special Task Force selected by the secretary for Health, Education and Welfare, they prepared a report under the title "Work in America" which was undertaken to investigate the worrisome dissatisfaction of American workers with their jobs. The authors of this study came to be conclusion that the effects of Taylor's Scientific Management techniques were a significant factor in the alienation and the disenchantment of blue-collar workers.[128] Bukowski not only acknowledges the existence of this alienated disenchanted form of labour but he refuses to accept that the situation is normal. In a letter to John William Corrington, Bukowski describes working for the U.S. Post Office, as a "continual hell of doing an idiot boring searing task at a rate almost beyond bodily endurance, and, getting paid very little."[129] Bukowski's comments are characteristic of the new class of worker that was emerging during the 1960's, namely, a more educated worker who was no longer happy to accept the rigid bureaucracy of industry.

Throughout the novels *Factotum* (1975) and *Post Office* (1971), Bukowski effectively demonstrates how work has come to serve as a means of social control, illustrating that Fordism and Taylorism are still practised. Gramsci explains how managers increasingly sought to control the workforce, sighting the attempts

---

[127] Braverman, H. *Labour and Monopoly Capital, The Degradation of Work in the Twentieth Century*. (New York: Monthly Review Press, 1975). pp. 85-92.
[128] Harrison, R. *Against the American Dream, Essays on Charles Bukowski*. (Santa Rosa: Black Sparrow Press, 1995), p. 131.
[129] Cooney, S. (ed). *Charles Bukowski, Living on Luck – selected letters 1960's-1970's, volume 2*. (Santa Rosa: Black Sparrow Press, 1995). p. 54.

made by Ford, with a body of inspectors, "to intervene in the private lives of his employees and to control how they spent their wages," emphasising that "someone who works for a fixed wage, with fixed hours, does not have time to dedicate himself to the pursuit of drink or to sport or to evade the law."[130] When commenting upon Frederick Taylor's methods of scientific management, Gramsci wrote, that in order to produce and maintain a new form of mechanical worker additional mechanisms of control were needed to extend beyond the work place and into the workers personal life. Therefore, Gramsci saw the introduction of Prohibition in America not as a means from which the Puritan strain of American civilization could control the working man's desire for leisure activities such as: drinking and womanizing, but more as a means from which to ensure that the new industrialized worker was not wasting time and energy pursuing activities that were not profitable.[131]

The novel *Factotum* (1975) follows Henry Chinaski for over a decade as he travels across America drifting from one dead end job to the next. This hand to mouth existence enables Bukowski to illustrate how work has enslaved the lives of workers. Therefore, *Factotum* is centrally about work, and more importantly, the refusal of work. Bukowski's representation of numerous horrible soul destroying jobs reinforces the dead end impression of the pointlessness of labour. Therefore, *Factotum* illustrates that jobs are horrible as opposed to simply having a horrible job. In the second chapter of *Factotum* Henry Chinaski explains:

> "I remember how my father used to come home each night
> and talk about his job to my mother. The job talk began
> when he entered the door, continued over the dinner table,

---

[130] Harrison, R. *Against the American Dream, Essays on Charles Bukowski*. (Santa Rosa: Black Sparrow Press, 1995), p. 137.
[131] *Ibid*, p. 127.

and ended in the bedroom where my father would scream "Lights Out!" at 8 p.m., so he could get his rest and his full strength for the job the next day. There was no other subject except the job."[132]

The significance of the job is repeated again in the novel *Ham on Rye* (1982), here Henry Chinaski remembers, "my father was talking about his job, as always."…"he talked to my mother about his "job" from the moment he entered the door in the evenings until he slept. He was determined to rise in the ranks."[133] Bukowski describes how the job has become a subject of primary importance intruding into one's life, causing an otherwise tolerable existence, to become hell. Bukowski also illustrates how an individual's self-esteem becomes closely connected to the world of work, as his character Chinaski explains in *Ham on Rye*:

"My mother went to her low-paying job each morning and my father, who didn't have a job, left each morning too. Although most of the neighbors were unemployed he didn't want them to think he was jobless. So he got into his car each morning at the same time and drove off as if he were going to work."[134]

Through this observation Bukowski is able to portray how the job deforms people and in turn affects their social behaviour and relationships in a negative manner. In this case Henry Chinaski's father later becomes physically abusive towards his family due to the frustration of not having a job. From this perspective the world of work becomes more than just an activity and a means to acquire wealth. It

---

[132] Bukowski, C. *Factotum*. (London: Virgin Publishing Ltd, 1996), p. 17.
[133] Bukowski, C. *Ham on Rye*. (Santa Rosa: Black Sparrow Press, 1996), p. 41, 152.
[134] *Ibid*, p.113.

dominates every aspect of an individual's life, determining the value of their identity and their sense of worth.

Charles Bukowski explores how the bureaucracy of the work place has created systems of hierarchy that are often abusive and unreasonable toward the worker. In *Post Office* (1971) he introduces Jonstone the "Stone" who right from the beginning is described as being trouble, "The soup was a bullneck named Jonstone…Jonstone liked to wear dark-red shirts-that meant danger and blood."[135] Bukowski describes how individuals like Jonstone are able to operate within the system explaining, "The subs themselves made Jonston possible by obeying his impossible orders. I couldn't see how a man of such obvious cruelty could be allowed to have his position."[136] But when Bukowski's character, Chinaski, files a thirty page complaint against "The Stone" on his day off, Chinaski comes up against the systems hierarchy where management instantly dismiss his complaint. In addition to screaming words of profanity at Chinaski the management become unreasonable, using the excuse, "MR. JONSTONE IS A FINE MAN"…he…"HAS BEEN WITH THE POST OFFICE FOR 30 YEARS!"[137] What follows is Jonstone's continuous harassment towards Chinaski by giving him harder routes and writing him up for minor infractions. Here Bukowski effectively illustrates how "the management" will often condone forms of bullying, especially if it works in the interest of productivity.

Bukowski illustrates the futile struggle that the individual worker has in trying to acquire fair treatment in a system which is clearly not designed to do so. This is because management systems tend to set up procedures or mechanisms of "fairness" that cannot truly be put into practice, as they would necessitate giving workers real power, which would not work in the long term interests of

---

[135] Bukowski, C. *Post Office*. (London: Virgin Publishing Ltd, 1996). p. 8.
[136] *Ibid*, p. 9.
[137] *Ibid*, p. 10.

Bukowski and the Beats

management. Another reason why the worker is easy to exploit is the fact that there exists a complete lack of solidarity among workers, Bukowski explores this through the character G.G., who "had been a carrier since his early twenties and now was in his late sixties."[138] G.G. has been unfairly accused of child molestation placing him under great anxiety which later begins to effect his performance. One day G.G. being unable to pack his mail sack in time as a result of a last minute addition of circular's, "put his head down in his arms and began to cry softly."[139] After running into the locker room G.G. is never to return to work again. Chinaski makes some attempt to show concern:

> "hey," I said a couple of times, "hey!"
> But they wouldn't look at G.G.
> I walked over to G.G. Touched him on the arm:
> "G.G.," I said, "what can I do for you?"[140]

But the rest of the workers show no interest at all, and after G.G. has gone they never mention his name again. By using this example Bukowski illustrates just how expendable the work force has become, and in turn, how apathetic the worker's attitude has become towards his fellow colleagues. Without any sense of comradeship or solidarity the worker has no attachment to his fellow peers and therefore sees no need in assisting a colleague or providing moral support.

One of the reasons why the workforce has become so expendable, with workers adopting an apathetic attitude, is due to a lack of representation by trade unions. Consequently there exists no collective refusal to work as Bukowski explains in *Post Office* (1971) when saying "the union man was worthless."[141] Bukowski has expanded upon this theme in the novel *Ham on Rye* (1982). After

---

[138] Bukowski, C. *Post Office*. (London: Virgin Publishing Ltd, 1996). p. 34.
[139] *Ibid*, p. 37.
[140] *Ibid*, p. 38.
[141] *Ibid*, p. 9.

Henry Chinaski finds a job as a stockclerk working at Mears-Starbuck, the Superintendent Mr Ferris explains to him during an induction meeting, "your starting salary is forty-four-and-a-half cents an hour. We are non-union here. Management believes that what is fair for the company is fair for you. We are like a family, dedicated to serve and to profit."[142] With regards to the attitudes of American workers Harrison notes that, "...because of their individualist nature. There is no instance of any kind of collective refusal..."[143] This effectively results in the workforce becoming increasingly divided and is therefore more susceptible to forms of exploitation.

Gabriel Kolko argues that trade unions have preferred to remain aloof from supporting worker's rights and instead have pursued their own interests. When analysing America's labour unions Kolko states, "the fact remains that American unions have found it infinitely simpler to adjust to capitalism, or even to help manage it within their own industry, than to replace it."[144] While Aronowitz has noted, that "the wildcat strike of postal workers in 1970 took place over the heads of the union leadership and became a national strike without central coordination or direction."[145] Clearly there is an element of collusion and alliance existing between business and organized labour. The Centre for the Study of Democratic Institutions in America published a paper titled, "Labour Looks at Labour" (1963), this study concluded, "what has happened is that the union has become almost indistinguishable in its own eyes from the corporation. We see the phenomenon today of unions and corporations jointly lobbying."[146]

---

[142] Bukowski, C. *Ham on Rye*. (Santa Rosa: Black Sparrow Press, 1996), p. 205.
[143] Harrison, R. *Against the American Dream, Essays on Charles Bukowski*. (Santa Rosa: Black Sparrow Press, 1995), p. 150.
[144] *Ibid*, p. 150.
[145] *Ibid*, p. 151.
[146] Marcuse, H. *One Dimensional Man, Studies in the Ideology of Advanced Industrial Society*. (London: Routledge and Kegan Paul Ltd, 1968). pp. 19-20.

Bukowski and the Beats

The result of this is that a union is not going to be able to convince workers that the company they work for is a separate concern when both the union and the corporation are out lobbying for bigger contracts.

Bukowski leaves the post office as a carrier only to return again as a clerk this enables the novel *Post Office* (1971) to offer a broader critique of the work within a bureaucracy. Although the work of a postal clerk is not as physical as that of a carrier, Harrison insists that it is nevertheless debilitating, as the work is extremely routine and requires repetitive movement which must be endured for exceedingly long periods of time.[147] In *Post Office* Bukowski observes how the management has gained increasing levels of control over the worker with oppressive supervisors and irrational work rules. He describes the restrictive conditions explaining how there was "No talking allowed. Two 10 minute breaks in 8 hours. They wrote down the time when you left and the time when you came back. If you stayed 12 or 13 minutes, you heard about it."[148] Later in the novel Bukowski describes how the worker deteriorates and becomes disfigured, due to the debilitating conditions of working over long periods of time:

> "They either melted," he explains, "or they got fat, huge, especially around the ass and the belly. It was the stool and the same motion and the same talk. And there I was, dizzy spells and pains in my arms, neck, chest everywhere. I slept all day resting up for the job. On weekends I had to drink to forget it."[149]

According to Harrison, the ever-increasing technological efficiency of the American economic system has put mankind at a point whereby

---

[147] Harrison, R. *Against the American Dream, Essays on Charles Bukowski*. (Santa Rosa: Black Sparrow Press, 1995), pp. 134-5.
[148] Bukowski, C. *Post Office*. (London: Virgin Publishing Ltd, 1996). p. 57.
[149] *Ibid*, p. 145.

human labour-power is no longer a significant factor in the production of wealth. Furthermore, mental labour has been collapsed into physical labour and white collar jobs, that had previously been different to that of blue collar labour, have become similar as the two have merged together.[150] Aronowitz illustrates this point explaining how "government employees, those engaged in retail and wholesale trade, and workers in corporate bureaucracies performing manual operations on accounting machines or typewriters, can hardly be considered radically different from industrial workers in general."[151] Bukowski has effectively reflected this observation in *Post Office* (1971), whereby the postal clerk maybe regarded as a white collar worker but as a result of technological efficiency has been reduced to the status of a blue collar manual worker.

In *One Dimensional Man* (1964), Marcuse indicates that human labour has been effectively divorced from the production of wealth. This argument is clearly explained by Karl Marx who states that, "automation in its largest sense means, in effect, the end of measurement of work...With automation, you can't measure simply equipment utilization." Marx concludes that "...there is no longer, for example, any reason at all to pay a man by the piece or pay him by the hour."[152] This results in the negative consequences associated with increased levels of automation, such as: technological unemployment, whereby a surplus of labour is created enabling industry to effectively keep employment costs down, and strengthening the position of management, whereby the worker becomes disproportionately weaker in comparison to that of his superiors.[153]

---

[150] Harrison, R. *Against the American Dream, Essays on Charles Bukowski*. (Santa Rosa: Black Sparrow Press, 1995), p. 128.
[151] *Ibid*, p. 128.
[152] Marcuse, H. *One Dimensional Man, Studies in the Ideology of Advanced Industrial Society*. (London: Routledge and Kegan Paul Ltd, 1968). p. 128.
[153] *Ibid*, pp. 29-30.

Bukowski and the Beats

Two examples from *Post Office* (1971) and *Factotum* (1975) clearly illustrates Bukowski's acknowledgement as to the separation of wealth and production. In *Post Office*, Henry Chinaski fails to sort a mail tray in the required time and is given "counselling" by Eddie Beaver for not keeping up with the production schedule. During this session Eddie Beaver insists that the system has been "time-tested" and therefore cannot possibly be wrong, explaining to Chinaski, "look, you took 28 minutes on a 23 minute tray. That's all there is to it."[154] But later in the conversation Chinaski argues, "if you're going to time a man, don't judge him on one tray. Even Babe Ruth struck out now and then. Judge a man on ten trays, or a night's work. You guys use this thing to hang anybody who gets in your craw."[155] Although not commenting on the separation of labour and production, Harrison does acknowledge the irrationality behind such methods, explaining "the problem with much performance evaluation is that everything that can be qualified is then used as a basis of decisions that also imply a judgement on quality."[156]

Chinaski attempts to defend himself using a rational argument, only he does not receive a rational reply. Chinaski's superior says, "All right, you've had your say, Chinaski. Now, I'm telling YOU: you stuck a 28 minute tray. We go by that. Now, if you are caught on another slow tray you will be due for ADVANCED COUNSELLING!"[157] Here Bukowski is essentially making two main points. Firstly, although the "system" claims to be rational using "time-tested" techniques, in practice, it is irrational and unreasonable. Secondly Bukowski illustrates how the work-place "democracy" is nothing more than just a procedure providing no real benefits to the worker. As Harrison explains, "Chinaski is allowed his "say"…but the counsellor "tells"

---

[154] Bukowski, C. *Post Office*. (London: Virgin Publishing Ltd, 1996). p. 146.
[155] *Ibid*, p. 146.
[156] Harrison, R. *Against the American Dream, Essays on Charles Bukowski*. (Santa Rosa: Black Sparrow Press, 1995), p. 136.
[157] *Ibid*, p. 146.

Chinaski, and that's that."[158] Therefore, what exists are mechanisms that appear, on the surface to be reasonable, fare and just, enabling the worker to believe that he has rights and is therefore playing an active part within the production process. But in truth these are all nothing more than cosmetic structures that in practice do nothing to provide protection and equality within the work place.

In the novel *Factotum* (1975) Chinaski gets laid off from an auto parts warehouse and is accused by the manager of not pulling his weight. In his defence Chinaski says, "I've given you my time. It's all I've got to give-it's all any man has. And for a pitiful buck and a quarter an hour."[159] By illustrating the in-equality of the capitalist system, Chinaski makes a distinction between work and capital by divorcing wages from productivity, stating "my time so that you can life in your big house on the hill and have all the things that go with it. If anybody has lost anything on this deal, on this arrangement...I've been the loser."[160] From the mangers perspective it is of paramount importance that Chinaski has not been working, but to Chinaski the act of not working is in fact meaningless. This is because when labour is divorced from production it is no longer the central cause for the generation of wealth, and therefore capital is effectively pushed beyond value or has no value at all. As the value of labour is now divorced from production, it can no longer be a mediation of the value of capital.

Chinaski says to Mantz, "I want my unemployment insurance. I don't want any trouble about that."[161] Here Chinaski's demand for unemployment insurance is significant as in order to be eligible for unemployment insurance one has had to have worked. But what is different here is that Chinaski expects to get his unemployment

---

[158] Harrison, R. *Against the American Dream, Essays on Charles Bukowski*. (Santa Rosa: Black Sparrow Press, 1995), pp. 136-7.
[159] Bukowski, C. *Factotum*. (London: Virgin Publishing Ltd, 1996), p. 112.
[160] *Ibid*, p. 112.
[161] Bukowski, C. *Factotum*. (London: Virgin Publishing Ltd, 1996), p. 112.

Bukowski and the Beats

because he believes, although he has not worked productively he has actually worked, and therefore by getting unemployment insurance he will get paid for not working at all. As Harrison points out this idea "goes against the grain of traditional socialist ideology, where work, and the worker, were glorified."[162] This marks a difference in the expectations of what the modern worker sees as his rights such as paid holidays and annual leave which did not occur in earlier proletarian fiction. It also conflicts with the basic ideologies of capitalism, namely that, labour and prosperity are dependent upon each other.

Unlike other Beat writers and followers of the counter-culture who often refused work and chose to live in poverty as an act of protest, Bukowski's refusal of work can be seen as a protest against the conditions of poverty caused by low wages. His rejection of the world of work with its mindless repetition and enslavement can be seen as a means of preserving the human spirit from further decline. Bukowski did not glorify the wage-worker in the same way that the Beats admired the Negro or the jazz musician, instead his writing serves as a critique on the developments effecting working-class experience. As a proletarian writer Bukowski was clearly ahead of his time, foreseeing the proletarianization of America's workforce before it became a recognised phenomenon.

---

[162] Harrison, R. *Against the American Dream, Essays on Charles Bukowski.* (Santa Rosa: Black Sparrow Press, 1995), p. 149.

Conclusion

The beats, according to Stephenson, have often been misconstrued as an endorsement or glorification of violence and nihilism, often encouraging the use of drugs, alcohol and promiscuity.[163] But what the beats have actually portrayed in their writing is a record providing an account as to the condition of the human spirit, reflecting the state to which society has become diseased.[164] They represent an opposition to the collective psychosis that society has succumb to by refusing to comply with its destructive madness. By helping to break down censorship they have broadened the appeal of literature by providing an alternative liberating vision.[165]

At the beginning of the 1960's American fiction was beginning to look historically outward, reappraising world forces and questioning what power did the individual have in facing them.[166] In seeking to understand the absurdity of contemporary society, through an assault on the historical and the real, writers often used what Bradbury describes as, "a cartooning of character, a fantasizing of so-

---

[163] Stephenson, G. *The Daybreak Boys, Essays on the Literature of the Beat Generation*. (Souther Illinois University: Carbondale and Edwardsville, 1990), p. 9.
[164] *Ibid*, p. 9.
[165] *Ibid*, p. 15.
[166] Bradbury, M. *The Modern American Novel*. (Oxford: Oxford University Press, 1983). p. 157.

called facts or actualities" in order to illustrate that history is itself fiction.[167] Doubting the value of rationality and intelligence, history was now portrayed as being beyond individual existence and reason, resulting in the modern world with its large structures of organisation and technology being portrayed as an apocalyptic threat to survival.

Such anxieties can be seen in Joseph Heller's novel *Catch-22* (1961), depicting World War II as a grotesque, absurd fantasy whose values could be applied to contemporary American life, while Ken Kesey's *One Flew Over the Cuckoo's Nest* (1962), has been interpreted as American authority, ruling and containing a madhouse through an oppressive regime of containment in which individuality is obliterated.[168] With the assassination of J. F. Kennedy and the escalation of the Vietnam War a sense of helplessness and horror caused much of the Post-Modernist fiction to become fantastic in nature. This provoked novels, such as, Norman Mailer's *The Armies of the Night* (1968) and Kurt Vonnegut's *Slaughterhouse-5* (1969), to examine the relationship between fiction and historical actuality in order to consider the ways in which reality is constructed and responded to.[169]

In contrast, Bukowski's work does not seek to explore historically outward, preferring instead to portray working-class conditions based upon personal experience. His depictions of marginal characters such as bums and drunks combined with graphic descriptions of blue-collar exploitation, appear to have foreseen the disintegration of post-War American life before it happened.[170] Today

---

[167] Bradbury, M. *The Modern American Novel*. (Oxford: Oxford University Press, 1983). p. 158.
[168] *Ibid*, p. 157.
[169] *Ibid*, pp. 158-9.
[170] Cherkovski, N. *Bukowski, A Life*. (South Royalton: Steerforth Press, 1997), p viii.

his portrayal of America no longer seems so obscure if one considers how the re-constituted Right became a dominant force in American politics during the 1980's.[171] With President Reagan's promise to middle-class suburbanites that he would trim social programmes, cut taxes and bring inflation under control, despite the cost in terms of blue-collar employment, effectively resulted in millions of workings-class Americans becoming unemployed.[172]

Bukowski's descriptions of skid row with its rooming houses and run-down seedy bars is no longer a way of life exclusively endured by disadvantaged minority figures living at the lower end of the socio-economic spectrum. His portrayal of a nomadic aimless existence, searching for low paid, unskilled, temporary forms of employment in *Factotum* (1975), has become a typical existence for many in today's society, while the depiction and rejection of his dysfunctional family in *Ham on Rye* (1982), illustrates many of the anxieties that are today common place. Although his critique on the conditions of work in *Post Office* (1971) may seem somewhat pessimistic and extreme, today's competitive workforce with its drive for increased efficiency and high output has created stressful environments of discontent, with abusive supervisors enforcing petty practice codes and demanding longer hours, many of today's workers feel exhausted, disillusioned and alienated from the production process.

According to the "Kerner Commission Report", America seems to have created two societies that remain separate and unequal, segregated from one another by an economic apartheid.[173] At one end of the economic spectrum the white skilled middle-class live in

---

[171] Lowi, T and Ginsberg, B. *American Government, Freedom and Power, Brief Fourth Edition*. (London: WW Norton & Company Ltd, 1996). p. 240.
[172] *Ibid*, pp. 240, 242
[173] Davies, M. *Prisoners of the American Dream, Politics and Economy in the History of the US Working Class*. (London: Verso, 1986), p. 304.

Bukowski and the Beats

sumptuary suburbs and gentrified neighbourhood's, while at the other end, an ever increasing low-waged deindustrialized working-class live in ghetto's and barrios.[174] As the globalized economy becomes ever more monopolized and increasingly competitive the trend towards increased inequality appears set to continue and the negative effects resulting from the degradation and exploitation of labour becomes ever more apparent.

---

[174] Davies, M. *Prisoners of the American Dream, Politics and Economy in the History of the US Working Class*. (London: Verso, 1986), p. 304.

Bibliography

Bartlett, L.(ed). (1981). *The Beats: Essays in Criticism*. London: Mc Farland.

Bottomore, T. (ed). (1991). *A Dictionary of Marxist, Second Edition*. Oxford: Blackwell Publishers.

Bradbury, M. (1983). *The Modern American Novel*. Oxford: Oxford University Press.

Braverman, H. (1975). *Labour and Monopoly Capital, The Degradation of Work in the Twentieth Century*. New York: Monthly Review Press.

Brewer, G. (1997). *Charles Bukowski*. London: Twayne Publishers.

Bukowski, C. (1974). *Burning in Water Drowning in Flame: Selected Poems 1955-1973*. Santa Rosa: Black Sparrow Press.

Bukowski, C. (1981). *Dangling in the Tournefortia*. Santa Rosa: Black Sparrow Press.

Bukowski, C. (1996). *Factotum*. London: Virgin Publishing Ltd.

Bukowski, C. (1996). *Ham on Rye*. Santa Rosa: Black Sparrow Press.

Bukowski, C. (1996). *Hollywood*. Santa Rosa: Black Sparrow Press.

Bukowski, C. (1996). *Post Office*. London: Virgin Publishing Ltd.

Bukowski, C. (1969). *The Days Run Away Like Wild Horses Over the Hills*. Santa Rosa: Black Sparrow Press.

Burroughs, W. S. (1977). *Junky*. London: Penguin Books.

Burroughs, W. S. (1993). *The Naked Lunch*. London: Flamingo.

Cherkovski, N. (1997). *Bukowski, A Life*. South Royalton: Steerforth Press.

Christy, J. (1997). *The Buk Book, Musings on Charles Bukowski*. Toronto: ECW Press.

Cohen, A. "Divided Capitalism and Marx's Concepts of Politics." *Political Studies*, (March, 1995), vol 43, no' 1. Oxford: Blackwell Publishers.

Cooney, S. (ed). (1995). *Charles Bukowski, Living on Luck – selected letters 1960's-1970's, volume 2*. Santa Rosa: Black Sparrow Press.

Cooney, S. (ed). (1995). *Charles Bukowski, Screams from the Balcony – selected letters 1960-1970*. Santa Rosa: Black Sparrow Press.

Davies, M. (1986). *Prisoners of the American Dream, Politics and Economy in the History of the US Working Class*. London: Verso.

Davis, L. "Morris, Wilde, and Marx on the Social Preconditions of Individual Development." *Political Studies*, (September, 1996), vol 44, no' 1. Oxford: Blackwell Publishers.

Esterly, G. (1976). " Buk: The Pock-Marked Poetry of Charles Bukowski." *Rolling Stone*, (16 June), pp. 28-34.

Evans, M. (1975). *Karl Marx, Political Thinkers no' 3*. London: George Allen & Unwin Ltd.

Harrison, R. (1995). *Against the American Dream, Essays on Charles Bukowski*. Santa Rosa: Black Sparrow Press.

Heywood, A. (1997). *Politics*. London: MacMillan Press Ltd.

Hoffman, J. "What's left of Marxism?" *Politics Review*, (February, 1997), vol 6, no' 3. Oxford: Deddington.

Hunt, R. N. (1984). *The Political Ideas of Marx and Engels, II, Classical Marxism 1850-1895*. London: MacMillan Press Ltd.

Kerouac, J. (1991). *On the Road*. London: Penguin Books.

Kesey, K. (1998). *One Flew Over the Cuckoo's Nest*. New York: Barnes and Noble.

Locklin, G. (1996). *Charles Bukowski: A Sure Bet*. Sudbury: Water Row Press.

Lowi, T and Ginsberg, B. (1996). *American Government, Freedom and Power, Brief Fourth Edition*. London: WW Norton & Company Ltd.

Marcuse, H. (1970). *Five Lectures, Psychoanalysis, Politics and Utopia*. London: Allen Lane The Penguin Press.

Marcuse, H. (1968). *One Dimensional Man, Studies in the Ideology of Advanced Industrial Society*. London: Routledge and Kegan Paul Ltd.

Marx, K. and Engels, F. (1978). *Collected Works of Karl Marx and Frederick Engels, 1848, vol. 7: Demands of the Communist Party in Germany, Articles, Speeches*. (first edition). New York: International Publishers.

Marx, K. and Engels, F. (2011). *Economic and Philosophical Manuscripts of 1844*. New York: Dover Publications.

Marx, K. (1979). *The Class Struggles in France 1848 to 1850*. Moscow: Progress Publishers.

Marx, K. & Engels, F. (1985). *The Communist Manifesto*. London: Penguin Books.

Marx, K. and Engels, F. (1987). *The German Ideology: Introduction to a Critique of Political Economy*. London: Lawrence and Wishart Ltd.

McNaughton, N. (1996). *Success in Politics, A Comparative Study for Advanced Level*. London: John Murray Publishers Ltd.

Miller, H. (1965) *The Air Conditioned Nightmare*. London: Panther Books

Mouzelis, N. "The Left After Communism." *Politics Review*, (February, 1995). Deddington: Philip Allan Publishers Ltd.

Norse, H. (Summer 1994). "Laughter in Hell, Charles Bukowski is Dead." *ATOM MIND*, vol 4, no' 14 Albuquerque: Mother Road Publications.

Parkinson, T. (ed). (1970). *A Casebook on the Beat*. New York: Thomas Y. Crowell Company, Inc.

Purdy, J. (1970). *The Color of Darkness: Eleven Stories and a Novella*. New York: Bantam Books.

Richmond, S. (1996). *Spinning off Bukowski*. Northville: Sun Dog Press.

Smith, G. (ed). (Summer, 1994). "To Charles Bukowski – In Appreciation." *ATOM MIND*, vol 4, no' 14. Albuquerque: Mother Road Publications.

Stephenson, G. (1990). *The Daybreak Boys, Essays on the Literature of the Beat Generation*. Souther Illinois University: Carbondale and Edwardsville.

Tanner, T. (1976). *City of Words, A Study of American Fiction in the Mid-Twentieth Century*. London: Jonathan Cape.

White, S. "Needs, Labour, and Marx's Conception of Justice." *Political Studies*, (March, 1996). Oxford: Blackwell Publishers.

Woodiwiss, A (1993). *Postmodernity USA, The Crisis of Social Modernism in Post-war America*. London: SAGE Publications.

M. J. Poynter

About the Author

M. J. Poynter is an English "rogue writer" and underground poet. He was born in Reading, Berkshire in the summer of 1969 and spent his early childhood in the neighbouring suburb of Woodley. In 1976 M. J. Poynter's family emigrated to South Africa and lived for the next fifteen years in the small coal mining town of Witbank. The author completed his primary and secondary school education in Witbank during what he often refers to as "the thirteen wasted years". It was during this time that he developed an insatiable dislike for the apartheid regime and became heavily influenced by the counter-culture of the 1960's.

Novels written by M. J. Poynter:

Beatnik: Going to College in Durban, South Africa.
Middleburg: Going to School in Apartheid South Africa.
The Boston Curse: A Terrifying Tale of Dead Men's Fen.
Greetings from Ghana: An Englishman's Adventures
from the City of Accra.

In terms of literary style M. J. Poynter typically writes in a straight talking first-person narrative which produces a clear and concise description of events. The writer displays a sense of "dirty realism" with his gritty depictions of everyday life and social conditions. His works are autobiographical in nature being largely based upon real life events and combining an element of fantasy. M. J. Poynter's novels often portray himself as an anti-hero caught up in situations which are beyond his control. Themes of death and tragedy are combined with elements of the comic and the bizarre. The author often uses an interesting play on words to further convey a blatant sense of irony. His depictions of women are usually erotic in nature providing a sensuous mix of beauty and sexuality.

Printed in Poland
by Amazon Fulfillment
Poland Sp. z o.o., Wrocław